BREACH

IT'S TRUE,
IT'S TRUE,
IT'S TRUE

methuen | drama

LONDON • NEW YORK • OXFORD • NEW DELHI • SYDNEY

METHUEN DRAMA
Bloomsbury Publishing Plc
50 Bedford Square, London, WC1B 3DP, UK
1385 Broadway, New York, NY 10018, USA
29 Earlsfort Terrace, Dublin 2, Ireland

BLOOMSBURY, METHUEN DRAMA and the Methuen Drama logo
are trademarks of Bloomsbury Publishing Plc

First published in Great Britain by Oberon Books 2018
Reprinted 2020
This edition published by Methuen Drama 2022
Reprinted 2022 (twice), 2023

Cover photography: Front – Guy J Sanders;
Back – Richard Davenport, The Other Richard

Artemisia Gentileschi: the image of the female hero in Italian Baroque art © Mary
D. Garrard, 1989. Reprinted by permission of Princeton University Press.

A catalogue record for this book is available from the British Library.

A catalog record for this book is available from the Library of Congress.

ISBN: PB: 978-1-3503-2198-4
eBook: 978-1-7868-2661-9

Series: Modern Plays

Printed and bound in Great Britain

To find out more about our authors and books visit www.bloomsbury.com
and sign up for our newsletters.

CREATIVES

Director	Billy Barrett
Dramaturg	Dorothy Allen-Pickard
Set Designer	Luke W. Robson
Costume Designer	Kitty Hawkins
Lighting Designer	Lucy Adams
Dressmaker	Ronnie Dorsey (Edinburgh), Calum Harvey (Tour)

PRODUCTION TEAM

Producer	Ellie Claughton
Stage Manager	Rachel Pryce (New Diorama Theatre), Rike Berg (Edinburgh Festival Fringe 2019)
Technical Stage Manager	Stacey Sandford (Edinburgh Festival Fringe 2019, Tour)
Technical Assistant Stage Manager	Victoria Shannon (Tour)
Production Manager	Jack Greenyer (Edinburgh Festival Fringe 2019)
PR	Gregor Cubie for Borowski

THANKS TO

Arts Council England, David Byrne, Bryony Davies, Jon Claughton, Gregor Cubie, Marina Dixon, Aisling Galligan, Rosie Gray, Shelley Hastings, Kieran Lucas, Helen Matravers, Princeton Press, The Royal Shakespeare Company, Ralph Thompson and Sophie Wallis

PERFORMANCE DATES

Edinburgh Festival Fringe Previews
Theatre 503, London: 27th-28th July 2018

Edinburgh Festival Fringe 2018
Iron Belly, Underbelly: 2nd-25th August, 2018

London Transfer
New Diorama Theatre,
London: 16th October-10th November, 2018

Edinburgh Festival Fringe 2019 (British Council Showcase)
Cowbarn, Underbelly:
16th-26th August, 2019

Tour

Mala Voadora, English Family Festival,
Porto: 27th-28th September 2019

Cambridge Junction, Cambridge: 3rd October, 2019

The Spring, Havant: 5th October, 2019

HOME, Manchester: 8th-12th October, 2019

Cast, Doncaster: 15th-16th October, 2019.

Theatre Deli, Sheffield: 17th October, 2019

Nottingham Playhouse, Nottingham:
18th-19th October, 2019

Live Theatre, Newcastle: 22nd-23rd October, 2019

York Theatre Royal, York: 24th October, 2019

Square Chapel, Halifax: 25th October, 2019

East Riding Theatre, Hull: 26th October, 2019

The North Wall, Oxford: 29th October, 2019

The Pound Arts, Corsham: 30th October, 2019

Warwick Arts Centre, Coventry:
31st October-1st November, 2019

Salisbury Playhouse, Salisbury: 2nd November, 2019

Theatre Royal Plymouth, Plymouth:
5th-9th November, 2019

Wardrobe Theatre, Bristol: 12th-16th November 2019

Leeds Playhouse, Leeds: 21-23rd November 2019

Barbican, London: 31st March-9th April 2020

It's True, It's True, It's True was originally commissioned by New Diorama Theatre.

Notes on the Text

So, *is* it true? Yes and no. We've always thought of this show's title as both a statement of solidarity – an "I believe her" for Artemisia and the countless women who've come forward with accounts of rape before and after her – and a provocation: how much of what we're hearing is historically accurate? What does "verbatim" theatre – which typically aspires to truth – actually mean when dealing with a four-hundred year old court transcript, like the one we set out to re-voice? Hand-written by notaries whilst the testimonies were given, it was later discovered, patched together, transcribed and translated several times before even reaching our rehearsal room.

We took those existing interferences and the – in some cases, literal – holes in this document as a theatrical invitation, just like the recorded words themselves. An invitation, that is, to re-order and re-word testimonies, to discard and fabricate episodes, to devise flashback sequences and even dramatise Gentileschi's paintings as their own form of "evidence". So it's now difficult to pinpoint in this playtext where documented history ends and our own imaginations begin. "Truth", then, is tricky even before getting to the events disputed by the characters in the play.

It still feels necessary, though, to clarify here some of the liberties we've taken with the recorded court proceedings, largely due to the limits of an hour-long three-hander. Tuzia, for example, has been conflated with another neighbour, Giovan Battista Stiatessi, who gave important evidence in Artemisia's favour. The circumstances and motives behind the theft of Artemisia's painting have also been altered for narrative clarity. Perhaps our most striking omission to those familiar with this story is the revelation that Tassi was in fact married, and may have had his wife assassinated after he committed adultery with her sister. This subplot and further details can be found in the transcript itself, indexed in Mary D. Garrard's *Artemisia Gentileschi: The Image of the Female Hero in Italian Baroque Art.*

But some passages of that document demanded to be left intact, sacred. Artemisia's account of the rape remains largely unchanged, as does her exchange with Tassi when he was allowed to cross-examine her, and when tortured she did indeed repeat the phrase "it is true". It was this voice – already bold, visionary and uncompromising at only seventeen years old – that inspired us throughout the making of this show, in a room filled with the rage, tears, laughter and love of a similarly impassioned creative team. Just as the artists of Gentileschi's time imagined and painted biblical figures in the clothes and buildings of their own societies, so we heard Artemisia speak to us directly in the 21st Century. We hope that in reading, watching or performing this text, you'll hear her loud and clear.

Staging

We took the 1612 transcript as an incomplete record of a historical event, as well as a blueprint for performance – and similarly, here we've tried to present this playtext as both a written rendering of our own show and an outline for future productions – should anyone wish to stage one.

Stage directions are therefore intended as descriptive, rather than prescriptive – painting a picture of our own decisions and design elements. For context: our playing space is designed as both a courtroom and an artist's studio, with step ladders that fold into chairs and tables standing in for legal benches and witness boxes, and a paint trolley wheeling out for Susanna's garden and Holofernes' bed. Our costumes clash together the historical and the contemporary, with sharp jackets and outsized cuffs and collars contrasting with velvet cloaks, fake beards and ornate dresses. Music – baroque, punk and contemporary – was integral to creating our show, so we've provided a track listing throughout.

It's True, It's True, It's True was devised as an all-female, multi-roling three-hander – with actors snappily switching characters and rotating the part of the Judge.

[Zefirno torna e di soavi accenti, SV 251 – Claudio Monteverdi]

PROLOGUE

[Vespers of 1610, Magnificat (High) – Claudio Monteverdi]

Voice-over plays over a dark stage.

TASSI: Rome, 1612.

A courtroom.

The questions are asked in Latin, and the answers given in Italian.

Each testimony of the seven-month trial is written down. But not all of the pages survive.

What remains, four centuries later, is translated into English, and now will be spoken again.

Everything that follows is true.

SCENE ONE

[Born Free – MIA]

The cast enter purposefully in single file, then perform a slowed-down, distorted jig, the kind seen in traditional Shakespeare performances, before taking their places in the courtroom. Between each fragment in this scene, the music Born Free returns as the cast rotate around the court, alternating the role of the Judge.

TUZIA raises her right hand as if swearing on a Bible.

TUZIA: I was taken last Friday evening from my house at the entrance of Santo Spirito, at about eleven o'clock, and I can't imagine the reason for my imprisonment or this interrogation.

JUDGE: Okay, Donna Tuzia, we'll get there. First of all, how did you meet Orazio Gentileschi?

TUZIA: I've known Signor Orazio for about a year, since he lived across the street from me in Via Margutta.

JUDGE: And what about his daughter, Artemisia Gentileschi?

TUZIA: I was told she was a respectable young woman, so I allowed my daughter to visit her. Later on, my elder daughter also began to associate with her, and so did I.

JUDGE: And how did you come to end up living with the Gentileschis?

TUZIA: Well, Artemisia and I began to enjoy each other's company very much, didn't we?

ARTEMISIA goes to speak – TUZIA cuts her off.

She's shy. When Orazio saw us together he was so happy his daughter had become my friend that he actually hugged me quite warmly, saying now she could enjoy herself a little, as she was always alone and didn't have anyone. And he asked there and then if we'd take a house jointly and live together.

JUDGE: And how easy was it to move between your two apartments?

TUZIA: Very, sir. Signor Orazio had a door and a staircase built so I visited her apartment frequently, and she used to come to mine.

JUDGE: Who lived in their apartment during the time that you lived with them?

TUZIA: There were five in the family – namely Orazio, Artemisia, and her three brothers. Her mother died in childbirth, God rest her soul. Prudenzia, her name was. There was also a fellow named Francesco, an ugly type with long black hair whom they used as a model for the paintings. So, that's six. Sorry. I heard Artemisia and Orazio considered Francesco their enemy because he spoke ill of them, but what bad things he was saying I don't know.

JUDGE: And who did Orazio tend to associate with?

TUZIA: Signor Orazio had many friends, but there were two in particular. One was Cosimo, the Orderly of the Vatican, recently deceased, and the other one was called Signor Agostino who was a painter and together with Signor Orazio was painting a room in the palace. Agostino was a real gentleman and always showed great affection for Artemisia.

* * *

JUDGE: Signor Agostino Tassi, are you aware of why you've been brought before the court today?

3

TASSI: Can I just say, it's been eight days since I was arrested, and I was taken alone in the middle of the night? And no, I don't know, nor can I guess the reason I was arrested, or why Your Lordship wants to question me.

JUDGE: Please state for the court your criminal history.

TASSI: I've been in prison two times – no, three times. Once in Borgo, under the pretext that I had carnal relations with a sister-in-law of mine. I stayed in prison two days and then was released by order of the Pope, and acquitted with no requirement of payment.

JUDGE: …

TASSI: Another time? Okay, so – another time, yes, I was in prison in Tor di Nona for a triviality. You know that – Your Lordship was the judge and I was released immediately. Then, I was also questioned and tried in Livorno for having beaten someone up and I was acquitted, but I have not been questioned, tried, or imprisoned at any other time. Except for those times that I've just mentioned.

JUDGE: Please state for the court your place of birth, and your profession.

TASSI: I was born in Rome and I am a painter.

JUDGE: And have you always lived in Rome?

TASSI: No. I lived in Florence for a time. There, I got into the service of His Highness of Florence, with whom I travelled to see the world. I sailed on his galleys, and I did many paintings.

JUDGE: Very impressive.

TASSI: Thank you. Then I returned here to Rome.

JUDGE: How was it that you came to know Orazio Gentileschi?

TASSI: I've known Gentileschi for a while, because he's also a painter. He painted with me at Monte Cavallo.

JUDGE: What about his daughter, Artemisia?

TASSI: His daughter … I taught to paint a couple of times.

Pause.

JUDGE: Do you consider yourself well liked, here in Rome?

TASSI: I do have friends, people with whom I usually associate and keep company. But now to be honest I don't know which ones are my friends and whether they are friendly to me or not.

JUDGE: Well, be clear for the court –

TASSI: Actually, no, I do wish to state who is not my friend now. His name is Orazio Gentileschi, and I declare that man to be my enemy.

* * *

JUDGE: Artemisia, could you please tell the court how you came to know Agostino Tassi?

ARTEMISIA: My father was a close friend of Agostino Tassi, who because of this friendship began to visit our house frequently, and became friends with Tuzia. It was her that convinced me to speak to him. She kept saying that he was a well-mannered young man, courteous to women, and that we'd get along well. She finally persuaded me to speak to him because apparently Francesco, a servant who used to live with us, was going around spreading scandal about me, and she said Agostino was going to come and tell me what the man was saying.

JUDGE: What did Agostino tell you Francesco was saying?

ARTEMISIA: He told me Francesco was boasting that I had 'given him what he wanted'. But I said it didn't matter to me what he said because I knew what I was: a virgin. But he told me that it was upsetting *him* Francesco saying these things about me, because of his friendship with my father and because he valued my honour.

* * *

JUDGE: Can we return to Orazio's daughter, Artemisia?

TASSI: Yep. I don't know much about her. Just Orazio told me that he had brought this woman *(Indicating TUZIA.)* in here with them with the firm intention of finding a remedy for the many troubles his daughter was causing him by being – I don't know how to put it – wild?

TUZIA: Yes

TASSI: Living a bad life. He was desperate and needed her to straighten everything out.

JUDGE: And did you ever speak to Artemisia alone, without Tuzia present?

TASSI: This I don't remember, sir.

JUDGE: But you were her painting tutor, weren't you? So doesn't that mean that at some point, you must have been left alone with Artemisia?

TASSI: I don't remember, sir.

JUDGE: Signor Tassi, please. Answer the question – Did you ever speak to Artemisia alone?

TASSI: I don't remember! I have no memory of it. This is ridiculous – I have other worries besides these, like the study of my profession and the amount of work that I have to do for the Pope.

* * *

JUDGE: Would it be fair to say that in the absence of her
    mother, you were acting as a guardian to Artemisia?

TUZIA: Yes. Well, whenever Signor Orazio left the house,
    he always entrusted his daughter to me to take care of,
    and expected me to notify him of the people who came.
    And he warned me not to speak to his daughter about
    husbands, rather that I should persuade her to become
    a nun – which I tried to do, several times, however she
    always told me that her father didn't need to waste his
    time because every time he spoke of her becoming a nun,
    he alienated her – so that was that.

JUDGE: Right. And what about outside of the house?

TUZIA: Well, whenever Artemisia went out, I always
    accompanied her. I remember one morning, I took her to
    church and we had to go at dawn, because her father was
    so jealously protective, and she said "Look, there he is."

    [Il Signore ti Ristora – Taizé]

    *All turn out to the audience, hands clasped as if in church. TASSI
    stares at ARTEMISIA's chest, who crosses her arms to cover herself.
    TUZIA whispers urgently for her to put them down. TUZIA then
    catches TASSI's eye and, thinking he's been watching her, waves
    back, flattered and flustered. He waves back coldly.*

JUDGE: And which church was this?

    TUZIA is still remembering the church scene.

    Which church was this?

ARTEMISIA: *(Impatiently.)* Santo Giovanni.

TUZIA: Santo Giovanni, that's right, yes, at dawn –

7

ARTEMISIA: And there, outside the church, I saw Cosimo and Agostino close by. Cosimo stayed back, but Agostino followed me.

TUZIA: Okay yes, and Artemisia said to me: look, there they are again! Agostino and Cosimo, let's go away. And Artemisia began to run as fast as she could.

JUDGE: So she stated she was uncomfortable?

ARTEMISIA: Yes. Directly, but it never made a difference. Agostino still followed me.

JUDGE: Could you wait your turn please?

TUZIA: Thank you. So I begged her not to run so fast because I couldn't keep up. We left and Agostino stayed behind and we went straight home. I don't think we saw Agostino again after that.

JUDGE: You don't think you saw him again, or you didn't see him again?

ARTEMISIA: I saw him again. Definitely. Because that day not only did he follow me home, he actually followed me into my house. He found me in one of my rooms and started complaining that I was behaving badly towards him and that I didn't care about him, and he kept saying that I'd regret that. And I answered, "regret what, regret what? He who comes here and talks to me like this must give me this, meaning put a ring on my finger."

JUDGE: Was this normal for him to just let himself in to your house?

TUZIA: No.

ARTEMISIA: Yes.

TUZIA: No.

ARTEMISIA: Yes! In fact, the following morning, after my father had left the house Agostino came again, this time with Cosimo, and Tuzia let them in. I turned to Agostino and said "you even want to bring that man here now", meaning Cosimo. And he told me to be quiet. Cosimo came toward me and told me to be nice to Agostino, and when I refused, saying I didn't appreciate being threatened, he said, "Artemisia, you've given it to so many, you may as well give it to Agostino as well." Enraged, I told Cosimo that I had little respect for the words of scoundrels like him.

JUDGE: How did he react to this?

ARTEMISIA: He told me to calm down, that he was joking.

JUDGE: *(to TUZIA.)* Does that sound about right to you?

TUZIA: Erm – I do not recall to that – maybe I wasn't there for that conversation.

JUDGE: So to your recollection, they followed her but didn't come to the house –

TUZIA: She's the one who said 'followed'.

JUDGE: What do you mean?

TUZIA: Could have just been walking in the same direction.

JUDGE: Didn't you say she was trying to run?

TUZIA: Yes, but I'm not sure there was anything to be running from.

JUDGE: So you're saying she's lying?

ARTEMISIA: They stalked me frequently. I was terrified to go anywhere, and then even scared to stay at home.

TUZIA: If I'm being honest, I think if they were looking at her, it wouldn't have been entirely uninvited.

JUDGE: So she invited it verbally?

TUZIA: You know how these young girls are. The power they have – say they don't like it, but it's flattering, isn't it?

ARTEMISIA: No, it's not. They were everywhere I went. Look, I painted this –

TUZIA: Course she did. You have to remember Artemisia was a fifteen-year-old girl. Young, creative, prone to artistic licence. Been on the other end of it myself.

ARTEMISIA: Can the court please consider one of my paintings?

JUDGE: Oh, so you want to move on now, to the alleged theft of one of your artworks?

ARTEMISIA: No, they stole my Judith and Holofernes. This is my Susanna and the Elders. I painted it around this time because of how I was feeling in all this.

TUZIA: What is this now, a gallery? Oh yes, alright, we've all seen it. Very rude picture actually. All bosoms and leering, no, didn't like that one myself.

JUDGE: Okay, yes I think we have that here.

ARTEMISIA: Do you remember what happens to Susanna in the book of Daniel?

TUZIA: Yes, Artemisia, we all remember the story.

SCENE TWO

[Marche pour la cérémonie des Turcs – Jean-Baptist Lully]

ARTEMISIA pulls down a large painted backdrop of the sky, replicating Gentileschi's painting, and undresses to her underwear to become SUSANNA, draped in a sheet. The other two become NARRATORS, and dress in the cloaks and beards of The Elders as they speak.

NARRATOR 1: There dwelt a man in Babylon, called Joacim. And he took a wife named Susanna, daughter of Chelcias, a fair woman that feared the Lord. Now Joacim was a rich man, and had a great garden joining unto his house, and every day at noon Susanna went into the garden for a walk.

SUSANNA wheels out the paint trolley, the back of which is painted as the garden wall from Gentileschi's painting, and continues to undress.

NARRATOR 2: The same year were appointed two ancients to be judges, and all that had any suits in law came unto them. The two elders saw Susanna in the garden every day, and their lust was inflamed. They perverted their minds, turning away their eyes, that they might not look unto heaven, nor remember just judgments, but watched diligently for her.

NARRATOR 1: One day, Susanna was desirous to wash herself in the garden, for it was hot.

SUSANNA washes herself, unselfconsciously.

NARRATOR 2: Nobody was there save the two elders, that unbeknownst to Susanna had hid themselves, and watched her. And the one said unto the other:

The music cuts out.

11

ELDER 1: So, shall we fuck her?

ELDER 2: Go on, then.

ELDER 1: Me then you, yeah? Or do you want to go first?

ELDER 2: Could do it at the same time.

ELDER 1: One in each hole? Always wanted to try that.

ELDER 2: Which one do you want?

ELDER 1: I'd go around the back ideally.

ELDER 2: I thought you might.

ELDER 1: Reckon she's up for it?

ELDER 2: Yeah, course she is – look, she's absolutely gagging for it.

The music resumes as the ELDERS slowly creep up to SUSANNA.

NARRATOR 1: And so the two elders began to stalk towards her. Susanna turned – but saw only trees *(She turns – they become trees)*. She continued to bathe.

NARRATOR 2: Susanna turned again – and this time saw only bushes *(She turns – they become bushes)*. So she continued with her ablutions.

NARRATOR 1: Until the elders, seizing their opportunity, ran unto her, saying:

The music cuts out.

SUSANNA: Oh God!

ELDER 1: Hi there.

ELDER 2: You alright?

SUSANNA: What are you doing here? The gates are locked.

ELDER 2: Just passing by.

ELDER 1: Admiring the topiary.

SUSANNA: Can you leave please?

ELDER 1: Woah.

ELDER 2: That's rude.

ELDER 1: We just wanted to talk to you.

ELDER 2: Yeah, we just came for a chat. You could at least give us a smile.

SUSANNA: I'm naked and you've been watching me. You're still watching me.

ELDER 1: Okay…

ELDER 2: Whoopsie-daisy. Sounds like someone's built up a bit of a fantasy in their head.

ELDER 1: Voyeurism. Exhibitionism.

ELDER 2: Oh my God, is that why you're here?

SUSANNA: Sorry?

ELDER 1: Are we interrupting you waiting for a man?

SUSANNA: What? No, you've interrupted me having a bath.

ELDER 1: Wow, I can't believe we've just caught you cheating on your husband.

ELDER 2: What will the whole of Babylon say, when they find out they've got a new whore?

SUSANNA: What?

ELDER 2: Because you've been meeting another man here. Every day. Behind Joacim's back. Arse on the grass. Legs in the air.

SUSANNA: But that's not true.

ELDER 1: Who's going to believe you?

SUSANNA: There's no one else here!

ELDER 1: That's what we're telling you: there's no one. Else. Here.

The music resumes again, loudly, as SUSANNA and THE ELDERS take up and hold the positions from Gentileschi's painting, in which the Elders reach out for Susanna and she turns away from them. The ELDERS break out from the painting and resume as the JUDGE and TUZIA.

JUDGE: Artemisia, could you please clarify what you believe to be the relevance of this painting to your case?

ARTEMISIA: What do you mean?

JUDGE: Well this is an iconic image – it's been painted by many.

ARTEMISIA: Sure – but it's not just about the story, is it? It's about how you choose to paint it, what you make it say. Mine's completely different from the others.

TUZIA: Looks pretty similar to me. Same bushes. Same knockers knocking against the same Grecian sheet.

ARTEMISIA: Sorry, have you seen any of the others?

TUZIA: I've seen Alessandro Allori's. Honestly, it's identical.

ARTEMISIA: No. Allori's Susanna is encouraging. Look at her face in my one. Look at the angle of the body. It's pointing away from the elders, it isn't inviting their gaze at all.

JUDGE: Okay, yes –

ARTEMISIA: And it's turned away from the viewer, the presumably male viewer. *(Indicating a male audience member in the front row. The JUDGE tuts at him.)*

JUDGE: But she is, well, nude.

ARTEMISIA: No, she's naked. Because that's what people are when they have baths! The point is, in my painting you can clearly see that she doesn't welcome this, and I painted that because I know how it feels to be a woman who is watched, rather than a man who gets off on it! If we're being honest, Allesandro Allori's Susanna is clearly more like –

[Love on the Brain – Rihanna]

SUSANNA satirically sexualises herself like an ecstatic woman in a shampoo advert, or Barbara Windsor in Carry on Camping – whilst the ELDERS are ogling her more like Sid James and Kenneth Williams.

SUSANNA: Hey! I'm just gonna have a bath in my garden. I like to do it outside, because I'd hate for anyone to see me! Ooh! What am I doing now? I'm washing my hair. Oh! Hey, you boys. Stop watching me!

ELDER 1: If you were a gentleman you'd look away.

ELDER 2: *(Staring gormlessly.)* What?

SUSANNA: Well, at least don't come over here and ravish me!

ELDER 1: We wouldn't.

SUSANNA: You would!

ELDER 2: We wouldn't!

SUSANNA: Yes you would, you dirty old men! Don't you dare come one step closer, with your shrivelled pruney hands and your nasty, old dicks

ELDER 1: Your nasty old dick!

ELDER 2: My dick?

SUSANNA: – or I'll have to punish you – for being so lecherous.

ELDER 2: That's it – you're asking for it girl!

SUSANNA: Oh, noooooooo!

[Oh Bondage! Up Yours – X-Ray Spex]

THE ELDERS begin to chase SUSSANA around the theatre, Benny Hill-style – at one point running through the audience.

ELDER 2: Don't be such a tease!

ELDER 1: Come on Susie, give us a little!

SUSANNA: No!

ELDER 2: Just a squeeze!

ELDER 1: Come sit on my knee!

SUSANNA: Stop chasing me!

ELDER 2: It's been so long!

SUSANNA: I don't like to be chased!

The music lowers. THE ELDERS remove their beards and cloaks to become TASSI and COSIMO following ARTEMISIA home from church.

TASSI: Come here.

COSIMO: Come on Artemisia, be nice.

ARTEMISIA: I'm just trying to get home.

TASSI: Why are you ignoring me?

ARTEMISIA: I'm not.

COSIMO: Just let us in for five minutes.

TASSI: Is this how you treat me? I teach you how to paint and you ignore me in the street? You're embarrassing me.

COSIMO: Don't embarrass the man.

ARTEMISIA stops and turns out to the audience.

ARTEMISIA: And Susanna sighed, "I am straitened on both sides. For if I do this, it is death unto me, and if I don't, I cannot escape your hands." And with that she cried with a loud voice, and the two elders cried out against her –

SCENE THREE

Two midwives are on the stand.

SIGNORA DIAMBRA: I, Signora Diambra, have touched and examined the vagina of Donna Artemisia, and I can say that she is not a virgin. I know this because, having placed my finger inside her vagina, I found that the hymen is broken. I can say this because of my eleven years experience as a midwife.

DONNA CATERINA: I, Donna Caterina, have also examined this young woman. I touched her vagina and even put a finger in it, and I found that she has been deflowered since the hymen is broken. This happened a while ago, not recently, if it were recent I would recognise it. This is the truth.

JUDGE: Artemisia. You're seventeen years old. Unmarried. Please could you tell the court: in what manner did this occur?

ARTEMISIA: Now? With him just there? *(Indicating TASSI.)*

JUDGE: In your own time.

ARTEMISIA drops her sheet and throughout this account, slowly re-dresses: bra, shirt and finally trousers. She leaves her shoes and jacket off – she looks undone.

ARTEMISIA: Okay. One day, it was a rainy day, after I'd eaten lunch and I was painting an image of one of Tuzia's boys when Agostino stopped by. And when he found me painting, he said: "Not so much painting, not so much painting," and he grabbed the palette and brushes from my hands, and threw them around, saying to Tuzia: "Get out of here." And when I said to Tuzia not to go and not to leave me as I had previously signalled to her, she said:

18

"I don't want to stay here and argue, I want to go about my own business."

Before she left, Agostino put his head on my breast and as soon as she was gone, he took my hand and said: "Let's walk together awhile, I hate sitting down." While we walked, two or three times around the room, I told him that I was feeling ill and had a fever. He replied, "I have more of a fever than you do." After we had walked around two or three times, each time going by the bedroom door, when we were in front of it he pushed me in and locked it. He then threw me onto the edge of the bed, pushing me with a hand on my breast. And he put a knee between my thighs to prevent me from closing them.

Lifting my clothes, which he had a great deal of trouble doing, he placed a hand with a handkerchief at my throat and on my mouth to keep me from screaming. He let go of my hands, which he had been holding with his other hand, and having previously put both knees between my legs with his penis, his penis pointed at my vagina, he began to push it inside. I felt a strong burning, and it hurt very much. But because he held my mouth, I couldn't cry out. However, I tried to scream as best I could, calling Tuzia. I scratched his face, and pulled his hair, before he penetrated me again and I grabbed his penis so tight that I even removed a piece of flesh. All this didn't bother him at all, and he continued to do his business, which kept him on top of me for a while. After he'd finished, he got off me. When I saw myself free, I went to the table drawer, and took out a knife, saying: "I'd like to kill you. I'd like to kill

19

you with this knife, in my hand, because you have dishonoured me."

He opened his coat, and said: "Well here I am." I threw the knife at him, and he shielded himself; otherwise I might easily have killed him. But I wounded him slightly on the chest, and some blood came out. He fastened his coat.

I was crying and suffering over the wrong he had done me, and to pacify me he said, "Come here. Why are you crying? Give me your hand, I promise to marry you, as soon as I get out of the labyrinth I am in." And with that promise I felt calmer, because at least if he married me then I could have some sort of life, and have dignity. But obviously we're here now because that is a promise he has broken.

SCENE FOUR

TUZIA is on the stand.

JUDGE: Donna Tuzia, do you recall the incident in question?

TUZIA: I recall that one time Agostino came while Artemisia was painting a portrait of my son, and right after he came, she stopped painting. But she told me to leave her alone. So yes, I left and went upstairs to my apartment, leaving Agostino with Artemisia. But her brothers were also there.

TASSI walks up to TUZIA and grabs her by the hair.

But her brothers were also there.

JUDGE: So on that occasion, did you hear, or see, any signs of a struggle between Agostino and Artemisia?

TUZIA: A struggle? No. No.

TUZIA breaks free, leaving TASSI at the stand. He rips down the sky backdrop, and pushes the trolley away, making space for himself.

TASSI: Never have I had carnal intercourse, nor tried to have it, with Artemisia.

JUDGE: But, Signor Tassi, have you ever been alone with Artemisia in her house?

TASSI: While I was teaching Artemisia, I think that one time I was alone with her. But her brothers were always there.

JUDGE: And have you ever visited the Gentileschi household whilst her father, Orazio, was out?

TASSI: Yes. What do you want? I don't remember how many times.

JUDGE: We want to know why you were there.

TASSI: Because he had sent me there to teach his daughter perspective. I went a few times, and then I didn't want to go anymore. This is ridiculous, I've never been alone in Artemisia's house. I have nothing else to say – there is nothing else I can say. I have spoken the truth, and no one here can make be what has not been.

JUDGE: Alright, Signor Tassi. But we have heard that you visited the Gentileschi house frequently, even outside of your arranged lessons. So what was it you were doing there?

TASSI: Okay, so, one time I saw someone coming out of Orazio's house with whom the girl was flirting. So I went into Tuzia's rooms and said to her, "Tuzia, you know very well that Artemisia's father brought you here to look after her. Yet you tolerate people going upstairs in his house". She answered that she didn't know what to do as Artemisia would do as she pleased.

JUDGE: And why was it any of your business who was coming or going from the Gentileschi household?

TASSI: Because I was Orazio's friend. The persons that I saw –

JUDGE: Which persons?

TASSI: Obviously I don't know their names but I would recognise them if I saw them. The persons that I saw went for Artemisia, to screw her.

JUDGE: What gave you that impression?

TASSI: She told me. She told me. Once I stopped her on the street after she had said goodbye to one of these men, and I reprimanded her. I told her you should be a good girl, and not bring shame upon your father by falling prey to that behaviour that gave you the French disease, and by that I meant syphilis, and she said: "What do you want me to do? My father has led me to this. First when he was in prison for twenty days and left me in need of a loaf of bread; and second, because he wants to use me exactly as I were a wife." I told her she shouldn't say these things, because I didn't believe her – because I considered Orazio to be an honest man. At the time.

JUDGE: And this conversation between you and Artemisia on the street outside her house – was anybody else present for that?

TASSI: No.

JUDGE: So you were alone with her?

TASSI: Yes. But you said *inside* the house. Did you mean outside the house? Outside the house, yes– that one time.

JUDGE: Thank you. And what did Artemisia make of you checking up on her like this?

TASSI: Okay, I think I should clear this up. I was to pretend to her I was there for other reasons, that is to say I was to discover these intrigues by pretending I was attracted to Artemisia herself. Look – do you really think I'd be interested in a girl like that? Fifteen years old? Thinks she can paint? And she's a whore.

JUDGE: Alright, Signor Tassi – is there anyone else that can testify to this? Is there anyone who you can call as a witness to support this view of Artemisia's sexual reputation? Anyone?

SCENE FIVE

[Heard It Through The Grapevine – The Slits]

The cast mime grotesque sexual acts around the stage – humping the furniture, giving imaginary oral sex, etc., only stopping to become one of the witnesses. Each witness raises their right hand before speaking.

NICOLO BEDINO: Nicolo Bedino, former apprentice to Orazio. I just want to say I didn't get anything for being here. Not from Tassi or anyone. Listen, Artemisia is not an honest woman. My friend Pasquino said he'd had her before. I heard Cosimo say he was screwing her for three years. And I heard Stiatessi say she's a whore. Everyone's got bad things to say about her, apart from Agostino, who says he loves her ... but they've never done it.

MARGARITA THE WASHERWOMAN: Margarita the washerwoman. I saw Artemisia kissing various men at her house in Via Margutta. I'd often see her kissing Francesco Scarpellino, a painter, and when he'd come to the house they used to take each other's hand and go to her bedroom... but I don't know what they were going to do.

BERNARDINO: Bernardino, Orazio's barber, and sometimes model. When I was over at the Gentileschis' I often saw men retire to Artemisia's room. They shut the door, but they always came out red in the face.

GIOVAN PETRO: Giovan Petro, aged seventy-three. I've heard it said a number of times she isn't a virgin, but I don't know who made her that way.

MARIO: Mario, son of Filippo Trotta. Work in the paint shop. People always talk about her there, but I've never heard a bad word against her – just that she's a virgin and an honest woman. I've only seen her once stood shamelessly at her window.

MARCO COPPINO: Marco Coppino, ultramarine colour
mixer. People are always talking about her in the paint
shop, saying she's a public woman – that means she's
a woman who goes out in public – and that she's so
beautiful her father wants her as a wife himself, and he
likes to make her pose nude for other men to come and
watch. Basically he wants to fuck her.

The music lowers and the court resumes.

ARTEMISIA: Artemisia Gentileschi. No, I never had sexual
relations with any other person besides Agostino. It's true
that other men, including Cosimo, made all sorts of efforts
to have me, both before and after Agostino had had me,
but never did I consent. One time, Cosimo, he came to
my house after I had been with Agostino and made every
effort to force me, and because I refused, he said that he
was going to boast about it in any case, and tell everyone
I'd done it. Which he has done with numerous people,
including Agostino – who because of this, I think, has
withdrawn from wanting to marry me.

The music cuts out.

SCENE SIX

TUZIA is on the stand. She is disturbed by what she's heard.

JUDGE: Donna Tuzia, Can you corroborate any of these testimonies? Have you ever seen Artemisia with other men besides Agostino?

TUZIA: No. No one else.

JUDGE: And from what you saw of Agostino and Artemisia together, did you think they were engaging in a sexual relationship?

TUZIA: I didn't know whether carnal copulation had occurred because both of them denied it to me. But many times I saw Agostino alone in the room with Artemisia; she would be undressed in bed and him dressed. Sometimes Agostino would throw himself on the bed, and I'd find them laughing and joking together.

ARTEMISIA's bedroom.

TASSI: What's that?

ARTEMISIA: It's a painting.

TASSI: That's funny.

ARTEMISIA: It's my new painting

TASSI: What's it meant to be?

ARTEMISIA: Don't be rude. It's obviously a man, lying on a bed.

TASSI: Right, right.

ARTEMISIA: It's going to be Holofernes, but it's not finished.

TASSI: Okay.

ARTEMISIA: It's not finished yet – I need to change his face, and I know his arms are not quite right –

TASSI: Move out the way a minute. Who's – who's the model?

ARTEMISIA: It's Francesco.

TASSI: Francesco Scapellino, right.

ARTEMISIA: Yes.

TASSI: Did you pick him?

ARTEMISIA: No, he was just hanging around so I asked him –

TASSI: Sure, sure, and now here he is. Just hanging around in your room, looking over you.

ARTEMISIA: I keep all my paintings here.

TASSI: D'you like that? Do you look up at him there when you're on your own? Do you just go – *(touching himself)* "Oh Francesco".

ARTEMISIA: No. Stop!

TASSI: I'll leave you two alone then, shall I?

TASSI moves as if to walk out.

ARTEMISIA: Are you joking? Come back.

TASSI: I just feel a bit uncomfortable.

ARTEMISIA: Why?

TASSI: Are you going to change it?

ARTEMISIA: I just said I was going to –

TASSI: Who are you going to change it to?

ARTEMISIA: You. I wanted to do that anyway, I just needed a model –

TASSI: Good, good. That's fine. Otherwise I'd say you should just marry him.

ARTEMISIA: I don't want to marry him – I want to marry you.

TASSI: Oh don't say that. Do you know how unattractive that is? Do you know how much that makes me not want to marry you?

ARTEMISIA: Well, you have to –

TASSI raises a hand to emphasise his point. ARTEMISIA flinches, as if she thinks he's going to hurt her.

And I don't answer to you.

TASSI turns to face TUZIA, who is listening behind the door.

Or to that sad old slag who's always listening in on private conversations!

The court.

TUZIA: Sometimes I told Artemisia that I didn't like this hot pursuit of Agostino's, and she would reply that he was doing that because he had promised to marry her. I reproved her, in Agostino's presence, and she would say: "What is it you want? Mind your own business and don't meddle in what doesn't concern you."

JUDGE: Hot pursuit?

TUZIA: Yes, like the following and the turning up at all hours.

JUDGE: But I thought you said they probably weren't following her?

TUZIA: Did I say that?

JUDGE: You did. So which is it?

28

TUZIA: Well, now I think about it like that – I suppose, truthfully, in short, Agostino was always nearby. He was, so to speak, obsessed by Artemisia. Obsessed by the idea that other men were coming to Artemisia's house, to *screw her*, he'd say. When she was downstairs he would go to the entrance of her apartment to see what she was doing –

JUDGE: So I will ask again – did you let him in?

TUZIA: No! I mean not always. He would knock at my door so hard, I would at times refuse to open it. But he would threaten to do and say things. Tell me to shut up, that I was a stupid woman. Once he pulled me out into the street and pushed me into the dirt. He kicked me – kicked me on my arse like I was a stray dog. So yes, those times I would open the door. Out of fear.

TASSI: This isn't true! I've never had carnal relations with her. Artemisia's virginity – loss thereof – has nothing to do with me. Like I've said, she's a whore.

JUDGE: Signor Tassi, please.

TUZIA: Okay, I want to say something, which I thought Agostino by now would have brought up, but since he hasn't, I will. Agostino contacted me from prison a few days ago –

TASSI: No!

TUZIA: – and begged me to do him the favour of bringing Artemisia to him.

JUDGE: To his cell?

TASSI: No!

TUZIA: Yes! And when Artemisia and I came into the office of the Clerk of the Court, Agostino started to talk with her in front of me. He said that he was not a man who had ever broken his word and he didn't want to break it to her, that he

29

was ready to marry her as he had promised, before fifteen days went by.

TASSI: You are lying through your teeth, you silly bitch.

JUDGE: Order!

TUZIA: He said "If you want to get me out of this mess –"

TASSI: No!

JUDGE: Signor Tassi.

TASSI: This is bullshit. She's talking utter bullshit. What, am I supposed to just sit here, and listen to her talk about me like this? No, I can't. And I won't. She's a liar, she's a gossip, she is an informer and *(To TUZIA, lowering his voice.)* you're gonna regret this.

TUZIA: I have never informed on anyone in my life.

TASSI: Oh, except right now, when you're informing on me.

TUZLA: Your Lordship, he said that in order for them to marry, she'd have to get him out of this mess by retracting her testimony. Then he'd do whatever she wanted.

TASSI comes very close to TUZIA and shouts in her face, silencing her.

JUDGE: Signor Tassi!

TASSI: I'm so sorry.

JUDGE: Retract her testimony?

TUZIA: Yes, and then Artemisia said: "I don't want to do that". And Agostino said to her, well why don't you just blame somebody else for it, then?

JUDGE: Blame someone else? Like who?

TUZIA: Cosimo.

JUDGE: He's dead.

TUZIA: That's what she said. That's all I needed to say. I didn't want to cause a fuss, but I just thought you should know.

JUDGE: Okay, Signor Tassi. Signor Tassi. Do you want to respond to these claims?

TASSI calms and gathers himself, re-thinking his approach.

TASSI: Right, so, first of all, Sir, I ask you not to be offended by the lack of respect which I have shown in uttering those insulting words against Donna Tuzia here present. I did not say them to offend or show contempt towards Your Lordship or the court, as I honor all of you and I bow before you.

TASSI bows.

TUZIA: Oh, for god's sake.

TASSI: And God grant that she be equally honourable as to tell the truth when she speaks. I blurted out those words in anger, forgetting where I was –

TUZIA: It's a court of law.

TASSI: – but what she says is simply not true.

TUZIA: I'll tell you what else is true.

TASSI: – Here we go…

TUZIA: I know that Agostino and Cosimo forged an order to obtain a painting as though on Artemisia's instructions.

JUDGE: So this we know about, this is the theft of the Judith and Holofernes from the Gentileschi household?

TUZIA: Yes, the one with the man, you know, sprawled out on the bed. I was present when this took place. Cosimo wrote the note with his own hand in the name of Artemisia. I reprimanded them, and told them that they should not

31

take a painting of that sort away from a young woman –
but they stole it because of its likeness to Agostino, which
he was concerned would arouse suspicion.

TASSI: You are only saying this because of the words we
exchanged at Gentileschi's door. And you can wipe that
fucking smurk off your face. You're pathetic, aren't you?

TUZIA: I think you imagine that I am still a woman who
answers to you.

SCENE SEVEN

[Thursday Girl – Mitski]

ARTEMISIA is on the stand.

JUDGE: Artemisia, please could you assist the court in describing the painting that was taken from you?

ARTEMISIA: Okay. So it's huge. Life size. And it's dark, very dark –

JUDGE: And what does the painting depict?

ARTEMISIA: – very dark, but not a solid darkness, more like an endless space where you imagine things have the potential to emerge. Then from below there are these shards of light, which illuminate three figures. But they only catch fragments in the shadows – so, half a face, the tops of arms, locks of hair. A bed.

Two of the figures are women. And they're both in these rich dresses. One blue, one gold. And those colours together, they really contrast with all the blood in the painting. The blood pouring down the side of the bed. The blood coming out of this man's throat. The blood spraying out of his neck in this arc and landing on the women's arms and their breasts.

Oh, because these two women are beheading a man – did I not mention that?

The Judge gestures for her to continue.

One is holding a long knife in one hand, and with her other she's grabbing his hair and pushing his head down – that's Judith. And next to her, using both her hands and her full body weight to push him down on the bed, that is her maid Abra. And him. Naked. Barely covered by a blanket – that is Holofernes.

That's what you see: the darkness, the light, the women, the man, the knife, the blood.

The story's from the book of Judith. She slays the Assyrian general to free her city, Bethulia. And yes, everyone's painted it, but no one gets it right. Caravaggio's Judith is so – meek. She's got no power in her arms, and she looks like she's regretting it before she's even started. She makes it look like it's going to be so easy – like she'll be finished in a second, but I've seen executions – it's not like that.

When I was six, my father took me to see the execution of the Cencis. He held me up in his arms above the crowd so I could see the family led up to the scaffold. The son, Giacomo, they smashed his head in with a mallet, but the women, Lucrezia and Beatrice, they beheaded them with a small, blunt axe.

And the effort that takes – the exhaustion – I've given that to my Judith. She's rolled up her sleeves, and you can see her muscles pushing against her skin, because yes, he's trying to fight, writhing, but he can't even scream anymore. Because she's already got that knife halfway between his vocal chords, so any attempt he makes to scream just catches and bubbles pathetically in the blood in his throat. But she's just concentrating on cutting, cutting, cutting – on shutting him up completely.

Taking all that rage that she has been sitting in for
months, and channeling it into action.

The music fades out.

JUDGE: Right. So, are you saying that this painting is, again,
autobiographical?

ARTEMISIA: I'm saying I was angry after he raped me, yes.

JUDGE: And did you continue to see Signor Tassi for over a
year after he *allegedly* raped you?

ARTEMISIA: Yes, but what I was doing with him I did so only
that, as he had dishonored me, he would marry me.

JUDGE: May I suggest, Signora Artemisia, that it was clear
that he wasn't going to marry you, but that you were
enjoying this relationship?

ARTEMISIA: Enjoying it? No. And actually I was even more
certain about the promise of him marrying me as time
went on, because every time there was any possibility of
a marriage between me and another man, he personally
prevented it from developing.

JUDGE: And did you continue to have intercourse throughout
this time?

Pause.

ARTEMISIA: Yes. On many other occasions.

JUDGE: And would you say that this intercourse became
consensual, pleasurable even?

ARTEMISIA: I would say that I bled every time Agostino had
carnal relations with me. I didn't know much about that,
so I asked him, but he said it was normal for someone like
me with a weak constitution.

35

JUDGE: Were you in love with Signor Tassi?

ARTEMISIA: What difference does that make?

JUDGE: Have you told the truth?

ARTEMISIA: Yes. Everything I have said is the truth. If it were not the truth, I would not have said it.

JUDGE: And yet Signor Tassi claims he was never alone with you in your rooms.

ARTEMISIA: …

JUDGE: Can you please tell the court the manner in which the alleged rape occurred?

ARTEMISIA: What? Again?

JUDGE: Yes. But this time, look him in the eye.

SCENE EIGHT

The JUDGE signals ARTEMISIA to approach a table, opposite TASSI. She takes a moment to prepare before looking up to meet his eyes.

JUDGE: Please proceed.

ARTEMISIA: As I have told Your Lordship, last year during the month of May, Agostino used to frequent my father's house. He came as a friend and we trusted him. But one day he came to the house, and as I have said, I would never have believed that he would dare do damage both to me and the friendship he had with my father. I did not realise it until he grabbed me by the waist, threw me on the bed, locked the door and raped me, taking away my virginity. The struggling went on for hours, and no one came to help me.

JUDGE: Signor Tassi?

TASSI: That I have raped her is not true, nor that I have had relations with her. In her house there was a man named Francesco with whom you couldn't trust a female cat, and *he* was alone with her both day and night. And Pasquino from Florence, who boasted publicly that he'd had her. I visited her house with respect.

JUDGE: Would you be willing to confirm and substantiate your testimony under torture?

Silence.

TASSI looks to the JUDGE, and realises it is ARTEMISIA being addressed. Both look to ARTEMISIA.

ARTEMISIA: Me?!

The JUDGE begins to undress ARTEMISIA.

JUDGE: I propose a moderate use of the *sibille*. Thumbscrews.

The JUDGE puts a paint bucket on the table.

ARTEMISIA: But I'm not the one that's on trial here.

The JUDGE begins to undress ARTEMISIA to her underwear. There is a small but violent struggle before she finally relents.

JUDGE: Let me explain. The instrument is made of metal and ropes. We will wind these around your fingers and pull on them. Pulled tight enough, your fingers will be broken – tighter still and they will be cut off.

ARTEMISIA: I'm not the one that's on trial.

JUDGE: We appreciate that Artemisia, but we can't risk Signor Tassi's hands – he's a painter.

ARTEMISIA: I'm a painter.

JUDGE: For the Pope. This is the surest way to strengthen your case. Remove any mark of infamy.

ARTEMISIA: I have told the truth and I always will.

JUDGE: Then if you could please place your hands into the device, and repeat your claim for the record.

The JUDGE gestures to the paint bucket and ARTEMISIA looks inside it, horrified. The JUDGE takes her hands and forces them into the bucket. She looks TASSI in the eye across the table.

ARTEMISIA: I have told the truth and I always will. It is true. It is true. It is true.

TASSI: It is not true, you are lying through your teeth.

ARTEMISIA: It is true, it is true, it is true.

TASSI: Artemisia.

ARTEMISIA: It is true.

TASSI: Stop it.

ARTEMISIA: It is true, it is true, it is true.

TASSI: Stop!

JUDGE: Alright, alright.

[Plague – Crystal Castles]

ARTEMISIA removes her hands, shaking with pain, claw-like, which are covered and dripping with shimmering gold paint.

TASSI: Don't let her go, because I want to ask her some questions.

JUDGE: Go ahead.

ARTEMISIA: That can't be allowed!

JUDGE: I'm at a loss here, Artemisia. Signor Tassi, please proceed.

[Affection – Crystal Castles]

TASSI: Thank you, your lordship. First off, who made you testify against me, where did he approach you, and with what words? And who was present?

ARTEMISIA: It is truth that has induced me to testify against you and no one else.

TASSI: Tell me exactly how and with what opportunity I first had relations with you, as you assert, and where?

ARTEMISIA: I have said so much about that in this court, both about the time and the place that it happened, that I really think it should be enough.

TASSI: Tell me how I frequented your house. Tell me if anyone else frequented it, and who they were.

ARTEMISIA: *(To JUDGE.)* I have already spoken about how he frequented my house, and many people frequented my father's house, but no one came on my account.

TASSI: Tell me, did you father provide for your needs?

ARTEMISIA: Yes, Sir. My father provided for my needs. What do you have to say about that?

TASSI: Did he make you want for anything? Did he ever leave you alone with men in the house?

ARTEMISIA withdraws her hands in pain as if the thumb-screws have been tightened, splashing paint over her body and the floor. JUDGE signals for them to be replaced, and slowly she puts them back in.

ARTEMISIA: My father has never left me alone with any man.

TASSI: What about Francesco Scarpellino?

ARTEMISIA: I was never alone with Francesco Scarpellino, my brothers were also there.

TASSI: Did you ever tell anyone that Pasquino had deflowered you?

ARTEMISIA: When this Pasquino stayed in my house, I was seven years old.

TASSI: So?

ARTEMISIA: And I never said that he had deflowered me.

TASSI: Tell me, is it not true that a man deflowered you?

ARTEMISIA: …

TASSI: To what end, and with what hopes, did you give this testimony?

ARTEMISIA: I testified with the hope that you would be punished for the wrong that you did.

TASSI: Say why you were forced, as you say.

ARTEMISIA: Why I was forced to testify, or why I was raped?

TASSI: Both.

JUDGE: You can't ask why she was raped. Tassi.

TASSI: What protest did you make? Did you shout? And why didn't you make any noise?

ARTEMISIA: I've already said that when you raped me you held my mouth so I couldn't shout.

TASSI: What are the signs that a virgin shows when she has been deflowered? Say it, and say how you know it.

ARTEMISIA: I've said that when you raped me I was on my period and my menstrual blood was redder than usual.

TASSI: Have you told anyone that I deflowered you? Whom did you tell? To whom did you brag of it?

ARTEMISIA: I told my neighbour Stiattesi that you had deflowered me, but you had already told him.

TASSI: Why didn't you tell it immediately, and, if immediately, why didn't you bring suit? Why have you said it now and what induced you to say it?

ARTEMISIA: We didn't bring suit earlier because something else had been arranged so that this disgrace would not become known.

The JUDGE exits, and TASSI watches them leave. ARTEMISIA becomes aware once they've already gone.

TASSI: Were you hoping to have me as a husband?

41

ARTEMISIA: Yes, I *was* hoping to have you as a husband, but now I don't! *(She pulls her hands out, again splashing paint over herself and onto the floor.)* Look, these are the rings that you give me, and these are your promises.

TASSI leans closer and takes ARTEMISIA's arms, guiding her hands back into the bucket.

TASSI: Did anyone tell you that I would be your husband if you were to say that you were deflowered by me?

ARTEMISIA: No one told me this, but I have said it as it's the truth.

TASSI: In what manner did it occur when you were deflowered?

ARTEMISIA: No. No, I'm not saying it again. I won't say it again. I will not, and especially not to you, because you were there and you already know. I'm not lying. I'm not.

I'm not lying. I'm not.

This is true. This is true. I won't say it again. I won't say it again. It is true, it is true, it is true.

TASSI throws a bucket of water on the floor and leaves. ARTEMISIA shouts after him, to the court, to the world, looking everyone in the audience individually in the eye. At times she runs out of energy, but she finds the strength to continue.

It is true

It is true

It is true

It is true

It is true

It is true

It is true

It is true

It is true

It is true

It is true

It is true

It is true

It is true

It is true

It is true

It is true

It is true

It is true

It is true

It is true

It is true

It is true

It is true

It is true

It is true

It is true

It is true

It is true

It is true

It is true

It is true

It is true

It is true

It is true

It is true

It is true

It is true

It is true

It is true

It is true

It is true

It is true

It is true

It is true

It is true

It is true

It is true

It is true

It is true

It is true

It is true

It is true

It is true

It is true

It is true

It is true

It is true

It is true

It is true

It is true

It is true

It is true

It is true

It is true

It is true

It is true

It is true

It is true

It is true

It is true

It is true

It is true

It is true

It is true

It is true

It is true

It is true

It is true

It is true

It is true

I will say this forever
It is true

It is true
It is true
It is true
It is true
It is true
It is true
It is true
It is true
It is true
It is true
It is true
It is true
It is true
It is true
It is true
It is true
It is true
It is true
It is true
It is true

It is true
It is true
It is true
It is true
It is true
It is true
It is true
It is true
It is true
It is true
It is true
It is true
It is true
It is true
It is true
It is true
It is true
It is true
It is true
It is true

It is true
It is true
It is true
It is true
It is true

She plunges her hands into the water bucket, letting out a sigh of relief. She scrubs the paint from her hands using rags in the bucket, and once they are clean she stands up, tall and decisive.

ARTEMISIA: Okay, now. I need you now!

SCENE NINE

[River – Ibeyi]

JUDITH appears in a golden dress. She is a rockstar, a guardian angel, the embodiment of rage. JUDITH has cracked the world open and we are no longer in the court, but a new space that she and ARTEMISIA have formed together.

JUDITH: I am Judith – Daughter of Merari, son of Ox, son of Joseph, son of Oziel, son of Elkiah, son of Ananias, son of Gideo, son of Raphain, son of Ahitub, son of Elijah, son of Hilkiah, son of Eliab, son of Nathaniel, son of *some other dead old man.* The names of our foremothers may be forgotten but yours and mine will never be. Know why? Because of what I did on the night you painted me, Artemisia! You remember that?

ARTEMISIA: Yes.

TUZIA enters and helps ARTEMISIA begins to dress in a blue dress, so that tshe resembles Judith's maid Abra in Gentileschi's painting of Judith Slaying Holofernes. She touches her assuringly.

JUDITH: How thousands of years ago my city, Bethulia, was under siege by the Assyrians. So, I hatched myself a plan. man.

I washed my body with water, put on expensive perfume, combed my hair and dressed in my favourite gold dress.

I slipped sandals on my feet, adorned myself with bracelets on my ankles and wrists, rings, earrings, all my jewellery. I looked like fire!

And I said to everyone in the city: "Listen to me. I'm going to do something that will be

remembered for generations to come. I, along
with my most trusted servant, Abra, will leave
the gates of the city tonight. Don't ask what we
will do. We won't tell you until we're finished."
And as I walked to their city, I was arrested by an
Assyrian patrol.

ARTEMISIA: "Who are you? Where are you going?"

JUDITH: I said, "We are daughters of the Hebrews, and we
are escaping from them. I'm going to see Holofernes, to
bring him a true report of the situation."

*ARTEMISIA wheels the paint trolley forward, on which
HOLOFERNES is lying, drunk and babbling incoherently, barely
covered by a sheet. He sits up.*

HOLOFERNES: Who's there? I can hear you!

JUDITH: Holofernes. He's drunk. He's disgusting. Lie the fuck
down!

HOLOFERNES lies down, and JUDITH climbs over him, seductively.

And he brought me into his tent. I was left alone
with Holofernes. And before long, he was sprawled
out on his bed. And I went over to the bedpost,
near Holofernes' head and took down his sword.

*JUDITH pulls out HOLOFERNES' sword and licks it, mock-
seductively, laughing.*

And then I came closer to the bed, I grabbed the
hair on his head like this and I said, "Give me
strength today, Lord God."

[Vespers of 1610, Magnicat (High) – Claudio Monteverdi]

ARTEMISIA screams, a howl of rage. She runs forward and begins to strangle HOLOFERNES before JUDITH hands her the sword. She frantically beheads HOLOFERNES as JUDITH encourages her: "Keep going", "This is the toughest part", "Hack through the muscle, now bone".

Through a strobing, angular light and a haze of smoke, only fragments of the action are visible.

When she has finished, JUDITH pulls HOLOFERNES' disembodied head from a paint bucket and hands it to ARTEMISIA. She looks at it then holds it up, exhausted but victorious.

The music cuts. ARTEMISIA cradles the head. The women look at each other.

SCENE TEN

[Gloria – Patti Smith]

JUDITH: Jesus died for somebody's sins, but not mine.

Melting in a pot of thieves

Wild card up my sleeve

Thick, heart of stone

My sins my own, they belong to me

Me

TUZIA: People said "Beware"

But I don't care

Their words are just rules and regulations to me

Me

I walk into a room

You know I look so proud

I move in this here atmosphere where

Anything's allowed

ARTEMISIA speaks her epilogue over the music.

ARTEMISIA: The final pages of the court transcripts are missing.

But Agostino's false witnesses are exposed, and he's found guilty of my rape.

He's exiled from Rome … for a few days.

But then he comes straight back to work, painting for the Pope in the palaces and churches.

But I – I am the first woman admitted to the academy of arts in Florence.I paint for the Medici family.

I go to London and Charles I commissions me.

And I paint Judith slaying Holofernes at least seven more times.

I have a daughter, called Prudenzia, who I teach how to paint.

Yes, I was changed. I felt anger. I felt sadness. But I also felt happy, in my life. I put all of these things in my art – because I'm painting my experience.

And men would tell me I couldn't do that, that there wasn't an audience for it. And to them I would say: "as long as I live I will have control over my being. My lordship, I'll show you what a woman can do."

Artemisia comes back in with final verse, with the words changed.

We're at the stadium

And there's twenty thousand girls

Calling their names out to me

Marie, Ruth, telling the truth

We can all hear them

We can all see

We lift our eyes up to the big tower clock

And we those bells chiming in our hearts

Going Ding Dong, Ding Dong

Ding Dong, Ding Dong

Ding Dong, Ding Dong

Ding Dong, Ding Dong

Chiming the time when you came to my room

And you whispered to me and we took the big plunge

And oh, she was so good

Oh, she was so fine

And I've got to tell the world

That I made her mine, made her mine

Made her mine, made her mine

Made her mine, made her mine

The final chorus is sung, screamed and roared by all three cast members. With each "Gloria" the audience is blinded by a heavenly light.

G-L-O-R-I-A

Gloria!

G-L-O-R-I-A

Gloria!

G-L-O-R-I-A

Gloria!

G-L-O-R-I-A

Gloria!